Lily's Adv[enture]s Around the World

by Juliette Ruiz
illustrated by Bill Peterson

Scott Foresman
is an imprint of

Glenview, Illinois • Boston, Massachusetts • Chandler, Arizona
Upper Saddle River, New Jersey

Illustrations Bill Petersen

Photographs

Every effort has been made to secure permission and provide appropriate credit for photographic material. The publisher deeply regrets any omission and pledges to correct errors called to its attention in subsequent editions.

Unless otherwise acknowledged, all photographs are the property of Pearson Education, Inc.

Photo locators denoted as follows: Top (T), Center (C), Bottom (B), Left (L), Right (R), Background (Bkgd)

20 Charles O. Cecil/Alamy Images

ISBN 13: 978-0-328-51426-7
ISBN 10:   0-328-51426-8

6 7 8 9 10 V0FL 16 15 14 13

Lily Sung stared out the window of her new home in Chicago. "We're so lucky to be here," said Lily's mom. But Lily didn't feel lucky.

She had loved living in Korea with her grandmother and her parents. She had loved moving to Boston, where her mother went to college. She had loved moving to Los Angeles, where her mother went to medical school. When Lily's mother graduated, Lily was excited about moving to Chicago. That is, until Lily's parents told her they were here to *stay*.

"Chicago has many different neighborhoods," Lily's mom told her. "You'll feel like you're living in many different places all at once."

Lily wasn't so sure. Staying in one place and one city seemed like the most boring thing in the world to her. Lily's mother had encouraged her to write everything down so she would remember it. So Lily took out the diary her grandmother had given her. It was called an *il gi,* and many Korean girls had one.

"Dear Diary," Lily wrote. "Please let us move soon."

Lily's dad had lived in Chicago years ago when he was in college. That made him feel like a native. "I want to show you around!" he said.

Lily followed him outside. It was summer and very hot outside. "Remember how we always had to drive in Los Angeles?" he asked her. "Here, we can walk or take the local bus or train. That's much more fun, isn't it?"

"I guess," Lily said. She still wasn't sure how she felt about this new city.

They took the "L," or elevated train, to a neighborhood called Pilsen. Pilsen didn't look anything like Lily's neighborhood.

Everywhere Lily looked were colorful murals. Some of them had dancers painted on them. "This is the largest Mexican neighborhood in any city in the country," Lily's father told her. "Let's get an *enchilada* from this street vendor."

After they ate, they went to The Mexican Fine Arts Center Museum. "Did you know the first Mexicans came here in the early 1900s?" Lily's father asked her. "They worked in the steel mills."

6

Lily couldn't take her eyes off the paintings. There were large colorful paintings by Diego Rivera and Carmen Lomas Garza. There was also an exhibit of paintings of tiny little skeletons dressed up in all sorts of costumes. "Mexicans have a celebration called the Day of the Dead," said Lily's father. "They remember those who have died. They also celebrate the living."

They wandered back onto the street. All the walking made Lily hungry. "I want an ice cream," Lily said.

"We're not going to get just any ice cream," Lily's father told her. "We're in a Mexican neighborhood. So we're getting Mexican ice cream!" Lily's father bought two Mexican *helados*...mango for himself and papaya for Lily. "*Gracias,*" said Lily's father. That meant "thank you" in Spanish.

Lily and her dad passed kids playing in Harrison Park. They stopped at a grocery store. It was filled with all sorts of foods Lily had never seen before. Lily's dad picked up *chayote* cactus. "Maybe your mom can use this in some wonderful Mexican dish," he said.

"Did you have fun?" asked Lily's mother as Lily relaxed on the sofa at home.

"I did," she said. "It felt like we were in a city different from Chicago. I like feeling that I am not stuck in just one place."

"Well, then you will love our next visit," said Lily's dad. "I'm taking you, Grandma, and Mom to the Polish neighborhood!"

This time, when the family boarded the "L," Lily felt like an old pro.

"We're going to Archer Park," Lily's dad said. "Polish immigrants have been coming to settle in Chicago for many, many years. South Pulaski Avenue is the heart of their neighborhood. It's very social there."

When they got off the "L," Lily pointed to a sign in the window of a bank. "What does that say?" she asked her father.

"*Mowimy po polsku* means 'we speak Polish,'" he said. "Many people here speak only Polish. These local businesses help the community by hiring people who speak Polish too."

Just then, Lily heard some beautiful music. A young girl was playing a piano in the Polonia Book Store! "Piano lessons in a bookstore!" Lily said, amazed. The whole family stopped to listen.

"The study of music is important here," said Lily's father. "People support it just like in Korea." Lily could have stayed listening to the music forever, but her grandmother wanted to move on.

They walked past a beautiful old building. "It looks like an old theater," said Lily.

"It was," said her father. "Now it's the Copernicus Foundation Cultural and Civic Center. There are offices here and conference rooms to help support the Polish-American community."

"This neighborhood's big," said Lily. Her father nodded.

"The only bigger Polish neighborhood is Poland's capital city of Warsaw," he told her.

They walked past a church called St. Bruno's, on 48th Street. "This church holds services in the same way they have been done for centuries," Lily's father said. "Services are in Polish and English."

"Hungry?" asked Lily's father. "Let's go to Bobak's Grocery Store."

Bobak's had one hundred different kinds of sausage! There were *kielbasa, kiszka,* and *bolszewik* hanging from the ceiling. "Let's try the gooseberry compote!" said Lily's mom.

"First it was like being in Mexico, and now it's like being in Poland," Lily said. "There are so many different neighborhoods."

15

"I can tell from your expression, you want to keep exploring," said Lily's mother. Lily smiled. She knew how much fun it would be to take the "L" and walk to another Chicago neighborhood.

They got on the "L" and off they went. Lily's eyes opened wide. The streets were filled with *pagodas,* fish markets, and restaurants. All the signs were in Chinese. "We're in Chicago's Chinatown!" her father said.

At C. W. Mei's Gift Shop, Lily's
father picked up a *karate* outfit. Lily's
grandmother bought some ginger tea
at a tea and ginseng store. When Lily
saw people doing the slow movements
of *tai chi* on a street corner, she excitedly
tried a few moves herself!

Everyone was speaking Chinese, but
it didn't sound like the same Chinese
language. Lily wanted to know why.

"Ah," said Lily's father. "That's because there were Chinese immigrants coming here from many parts of China. Each group spoke different versions of the Chinese language."

Before they headed home, the family stopped at the Chicago Food Market. It was filled with bins of fresh fish. Chinese people were moving back and forth, looking for the freshest fish to buy. Lily's family bought some tasty fresh crabs.

Their last stop was Ping Tom Memorial Park. Lily saw a movie screen being set up. "They show movies here during the Summer Fun in Chinatown festival," Lily's dad said. "We'll come back another time."

On their way home on the rumbling "L," Lily couldn't stop smiling. "So," said her parents, "still want to move?"

Lily shook her head. "I have the whole world here in Chicago!" she said.

19

Ethnic Neighborhoods

Most cities and many small towns across the United States are home to "ethnic" communities. These are communities where people from a particular culture have settled. Did you know that Chicago has an old Swedish neighborhood called Andersonville? Chicago's Lincoln Square was home to a large German American population and still celebrates German heritage days. Chicago also has a Greektown that is home to the world's third-largest Greek community.

Some of these communities can change over time. The Mexican community of Pilsen first started out as a community of Czechoslovakian people who came from the Czech city of Pilsen.

See if you can locate some of these nations or regions on a world map.